Our Bucket List

	Description	Done
01	_____	☐
02	_____	☐
03	_____	☐
04	_____	☐
05	_____	☐
06	_____	☐
07	_____	☐
08	_____	☐
09	_____	☐
10	_____	☐
11	_____	☐
12	_____	☐
13	_____	☐
14	_____	☐
15	_____	☐
16	_____	☐
17	_____	☐
18	_____	☐
19	_____	☐
20	_____	☐
21	_____	☐
22	_____	☐
23	_____	☐
24	_____	☐
25	_____	☐

Our Bucket List

	Description	Done
26	_____	☐
27	_____	☐
28	_____	☐
29	_____	☐
30	_____	☐
31	_____	☐
32	_____	☐
33	_____	☐
34	_____	☐
35	_____	☐
36	_____	☐
37	_____	☐
38	_____	☐
39	_____	☐
40	_____	☐
41	_____	☐
42	_____	☐
43	_____	☐
44	_____	☐
45	_____	☐
46	_____	☐
47	_____	☐
48	_____	☐
49	_____	☐
50	_____	☐

Our Bucket List

	Description	Done
51		☐
52		☐
53		☐
54		☐
55		☐
56		☐
57		☐
58		☐
59		☐
60		☐
61		☐
62		☐
63		☐
64		☐
65		☐
66		☐
67		☐
68		☐
69		☐
70		☐
71		☐
72		☐
73		☐
74		☐
75		☐

Our Bucket List

76 _____ ☐
77 _____ ☐
78 _____ ☐
79 _____ ☐
80 _____ ☐
81 _____ ☐
82 _____ ☐
83 _____ ☐
84 _____ ☐
85 _____ ☐
86 _____ ☐
87 _____ ☐
88 _____ ☐
89 _____ ☐
90 _____ ☐
91 _____ ☐
92 _____ ☐
93 _____ ☐
94 _____ ☐
95 _____ ☐
96 _____ ☐
97 _____ ☐
98 _____ ☐
99 _____ ☐
100 _____ ☐

Bucket List Goal

01

_____

WE WANT TO DO THIS BECAUSE...

_____
_____
_____

TO ACCOMPLISH THIS GOAL, WE NEED TO...

_____
_____
_____
_____

TARGET DATE _____

THOUGHTS / MEMORIES

_____
_____
_____
_____
_____
_____
_____
_____
_____
_____

DATE ACHIEVED _____ LOCATION _____

02

Bucket List Goal

_____

WE WANT TO DO THIS BECAUSE...

_____

_____

_____

TO ACCOMPLISH THIS GOAL, WE NEED TO...

_____

_____

_____

_____

TARGET DATE _____

THOUGHTS / MEMORIES

_____

_____

_____

_____

_____

_____

_____

_____

_____

_____

_____

DATE ACHIEVED_____   LOCATION_____

Bucket List Goal

03

_____

WE WANT TO DO THIS BECAUSE...

_____
_____
_____

TO ACCOMPLISH THIS GOAL, WE NEED TO...

_____
_____
_____
_____

TARGET DATE _____

THOUGHTS / MEMORIES

_____
_____
_____
_____
_____
_____
_____
_____
_____
_____

DATE ACHIEVED _____ LOCATION _____

04

Bucket List Goal

_____

WE WANT TO DO THIS BECAUSE...

_____

_____

_____

TO ACCOMPLISH THIS GOAL, WE NEED TO...

_____

_____

_____

_____

TARGET DATE _____

THOUGHTS / MEMORIES

_____

_____

_____

_____

_____

_____

_____

_____

_____

_____

DATE ACHIEVED _____ LOCATION _____

Bucket List Goal

05

_____

WE WANT TO DO THIS BECAUSE...

_____
_____
_____

TO ACCOMPLISH THIS GOAL, WE NEED TO...

_____
_____
_____
_____

TARGET DATE _____

THOUGHTS / MEMORIES

_____
_____
_____
_____
_____
_____
_____
_____
_____
_____

DATE ACHIEVED _____ LOCATION _____

06

Bucket List Goal

_____

WE WANT TO DO THIS BECAUSE...

_____

_____

_____

TO ACCOMPLISH THIS GOAL, WE NEED TO...

_____

_____

_____

_____

TARGET DATE _____

THOUGHTS / MEMORIES

_____

_____

_____

_____

_____

_____

_____

_____

_____

_____

DATE ACHIEVED _____ LOCATION _____

Bucket List Goal

07

_____

WE WANT TO DO THIS BECAUSE...

_____

_____

_____

TO ACCOMPLISH THIS GOAL, WE NEED TO...

_____

_____

_____

_____

TARGET DATE _____

THOUGHTS / MEMORIES

_____

_____

_____

_____

_____

_____

_____

_____

_____

DATE ACHIEVED _____ LOCATION _____

Bucket List Goal

_____

WE WANT TO DO THIS BECAUSE...

_____

_____

_____

TO ACCOMPLISH THIS GOAL, WE NEED TO...

_____

_____

_____

_____

TARGET DATE _____

THOUGHTS / MEMORIES

_____

_____

_____

_____

_____

_____

_____

_____

_____

_____

DATE ACHIEVED _____ LOCATION _____

Bucket List Goal

09

_____

WE WANT TO DO THIS BECAUSE...

_____
_____
_____

TO ACCOMPLISH THIS GOAL, WE NEED TO...

_____
_____
_____
_____

TARGET DATE _____

THOUGHTS / MEMORIES

_____
_____
_____
_____
_____
_____
_____
_____

DATE ACHIEVED _____ LOCATION _____

Bucket List Goal

_____

WE WANT TO DO THIS BECAUSE...

_____

_____

_____

TO ACCOMPLISH THIS GOAL, WE NEED TO...

_____

_____

_____

_____

TARGET DATE _____

THOUGHTS / MEMORIES

_____

_____

_____

_____

_____

_____

_____

_____

_____

DATE ACHIEVED _____ LOCATION _____

Bucket List Goal

11

_____

WE WANT TO DO THIS BECAUSE...

_____

_____

_____

TO ACCOMPLISH THIS GOAL, WE NEED TO...

_____

_____

_____

_____

TARGET DATE _____

THOUGHTS / MEMORIES

_____

_____

_____

_____

_____

_____

_____

_____

_____

DATE ACHIEVED _____ LOCATION _____

12

Bucket List Goal

_____

WE WANT TO DO THIS BECAUSE...

_____
_____
_____

TO ACCOMPLISH THIS GOAL, WE NEED TO...

_____
_____
_____
_____

TARGET DATE _____

THOUGHTS / MEMORIES

_____
_____
_____
_____
_____
_____
_____
_____
_____

DATE ACHIEVED _____ LOCATION _____

Bucket List Goal

13

_____

WE WANT TO DO THIS BECAUSE...

_____
_____
_____

TO ACCOMPLISH THIS GOAL, WE NEED TO...

_____
_____
_____
_____

TARGET DATE _____

THOUGHTS / MEMORIES

_____
_____
_____
_____
_____
_____
_____
_____
_____
_____

DATE ACHIEVED _____ LOCATION _____

Bucket List Goal

_____

WE WANT TO DO THIS BECAUSE...

_____

_____

_____

TO ACCOMPLISH THIS GOAL, WE NEED TO...

_____

_____

_____

_____

TARGET DATE _____

THOUGHTS / MEMORIES

_____

_____

_____

_____

_____

_____

_____

_____

_____

_____

_____

DATE ACHIEVED _____ LOCATION _____

Bucket List Goal

_____

WE WANT TO DO THIS BECAUSE...

_____

_____

_____

TO ACCOMPLISH THIS GOAL, WE NEED TO...

_____

_____

_____

_____

TARGET DATE _____

THOUGHTS / MEMORIES

_____

_____

_____

_____

_____

_____

_____

_____

DATE ACHIEVED _____ LOCATION _____

Bucket List Goal

16

_____

WE WANT TO DO THIS BECAUSE...

_____

_____

_____

TO ACCOMPLISH THIS GOAL, WE NEED TO...

_____

_____

_____

_____

TARGET DATE _____

THOUGHTS / MEMORIES

_____

_____

_____

_____

_____

_____

_____

_____

_____

_____

_____

DATE ACHIEVED _____ LOCATION _____

Bucket List Goal

17

_____

WE WANT TO DO THIS BECAUSE...

_____

_____

_____

TO ACCOMPLISH THIS GOAL, WE NEED TO...

_____

_____

_____

_____

TARGET DATE _____

THOUGHTS / MEMORIES

_____

_____

_____

_____

_____

_____

_____

_____

_____

DATE ACHIEVED _____ LOCATION _____

Bucket List Goal

_____

WE WANT TO DO THIS BECAUSE...

_____

_____

_____

TO ACCOMPLISH THIS GOAL, WE NEED TO...

_____

_____

_____

_____

TARGET DATE _____

THOUGHTS / MEMORIES

_____

_____

_____

_____

_____

_____

_____

_____

_____

_____

DATE ACHIEVED _____ LOCATION _____

Bucket List Goal

_____

WE WANT TO DO THIS BECAUSE...

_____
_____
_____

TO ACCOMPLISH THIS GOAL, WE NEED TO...

_____
_____
_____
_____

TARGET DATE _____

THOUGHTS / MEMORIES

_____
_____
_____
_____
_____
_____
_____
_____
_____

DATE ACHIEVED _____ LOCATION _____

Bucket List Goal

20

_____

WE WANT TO DO THIS BECAUSE...

_____
_____
_____

TO ACCOMPLISH THIS GOAL, WE NEED TO...

_____
_____
_____
_____

TARGET DATE _____

THOUGHTS / MEMORIES

_____
_____
_____
_____
_____
_____
_____
_____
_____
_____
_____

DATE ACHIEVED _____ LOCATION _____

Bucket List Goal

_____

WE WANT TO DO THIS BECAUSE...

_____

_____

_____

TO ACCOMPLISH THIS GOAL, WE NEED TO...

_____

_____

_____

_____

TARGET DATE _____

THOUGHTS / MEMORIES

_____

_____

_____

_____

_____

_____

_____

_____

_____

DATE ACHIEVED _____ LOCATION _____

Bucket List Goal

22

_____

WE WANT TO DO THIS BECAUSE...

_____

_____

_____

TO ACCOMPLISH THIS GOAL, WE NEED TO...

_____

_____

_____

_____

TARGET DATE _____

THOUGHTS / MEMORIES

_____

_____

_____

_____

_____

_____

_____

_____

_____

_____

DATE ACHIEVED _____ LOCATION _____

Bucket List Goal

23

_____

WE WANT TO DO THIS BECAUSE...

_____

_____

_____

TO ACCOMPLISH THIS GOAL, WE NEED TO...

_____

_____

_____

_____

TARGET DATE _____

THOUGHTS / MEMORIES

_____

_____

_____

_____

_____

_____

_____

_____

_____

DATE ACHIEVED _____ LOCATION _____

24 *Bucket List Goal*

_____

WE WANT TO DO THIS BECAUSE...

_____

_____

_____

TO ACCOMPLISH THIS GOAL, WE NEED TO...

_____

_____

_____

_____

TARGET DATE _____

THOUGHTS / MEMORIES

_____

_____

_____

_____

_____

_____

_____

_____

_____

DATE ACHIEVED _____ LOCATION _____

Bucket List Goal

25

_____

WE WANT TO DO THIS BECAUSE...

_____

_____

_____

TO ACCOMPLISH THIS GOAL, WE NEED TO...

_____

_____

_____

_____

TARGET DATE _____

THOUGHTS / MEMORIES

_____

_____

_____

_____

_____

_____

_____

_____

_____

DATE ACHIEVED _____ LOCATION _____

26

Bucket List Goal

_____

WE WANT TO DO THIS BECAUSE...

_____
_____
_____

TO ACCOMPLISH THIS GOAL, WE NEED TO...

_____
_____
_____
_____

TARGET DATE _____

THOUGHTS / MEMORIES

_____
_____
_____
_____
_____
_____
_____
_____
_____

DATE ACHIEVED _____ LOCATION _____

Bucket List Goal

_____

WE WANT TO DO THIS BECAUSE...

_____
_____
_____

TO ACCOMPLISH THIS GOAL, WE NEED TO...

_____
_____
_____
_____

TARGET DATE _____

THOUGHTS / MEMORIES

_____
_____
_____
_____
_____
_____
_____
_____
_____
_____

DATE ACHIEVED _____ LOCATION _____

Bucket List Goal

28

_____

WE WANT TO DO THIS BECAUSE...

_____
_____
_____

TO ACCOMPLISH THIS GOAL, WE NEED TO...

_____
_____
_____
_____

TARGET DATE _____

THOUGHTS / MEMORIES

_____
_____
_____
_____
_____
_____
_____
_____
_____
_____

DATE ACHIEVED _____ LOCATION _____

Bucket List Goal

29

_____

WE WANT TO DO THIS BECAUSE...

_____

_____

_____

TO ACCOMPLISH THIS GOAL, WE NEED TO...

_____

_____

_____

_____

TARGET DATE _____

THOUGHTS / MEMORIES

_____

_____

_____

_____

_____

_____

_____

_____

_____

_____

DATE ACHIEVED _____ LOCATION _____

Bucket List Goal

_____

WE WANT TO DO THIS BECAUSE...

_____

_____

_____

TO ACCOMPLISH THIS GOAL, WE NEED TO...

_____

_____

_____

_____

TARGET DATE _____

THOUGHTS / MEMORIES

_____

_____

_____

_____

_____

_____

_____

_____

_____

DATE ACHIEVED _____ LOCATION _____

Bucket List Goal

31

_____

WE WANT TO DO THIS BECAUSE...

_____

_____

_____

TO ACCOMPLISH THIS GOAL, WE NEED TO...

_____

_____

_____

_____

TARGET DATE _____

THOUGHTS / MEMORIES

_____

_____

_____

_____

_____

_____

_____

_____

DATE ACHIEVED _____ LOCATION _____

32

Bucket List Goal

_____

WE WANT TO DO THIS BECAUSE...

_____
_____
_____

TO ACCOMPLISH THIS GOAL, WE NEED TO...

_____
_____
_____
_____

TARGET DATE _____

THOUGHTS / MEMORIES

_____
_____
_____
_____
_____
_____
_____
_____
_____
_____

DATE ACHIEVED _____ LOCATION _____

Bucket List Goal

33

WE WANT TO DO THIS BECAUSE...

_____

_____

_____

TO ACCOMPLISH THIS GOAL, WE NEED TO...

_____

_____

_____

_____

TARGET DATE _____

THOUGHTS / MEMORIES

_____

_____

_____

_____

_____

_____

_____

_____

_____

DATE ACHIEVED _____ LOCATION _____

Bucket List Goal

34

_____

WE WANT TO DO THIS BECAUSE...

_____

_____

_____

TO ACCOMPLISH THIS GOAL, WE NEED TO...

_____

_____

_____

_____

TARGET DATE _____

THOUGHTS / MEMORIES

_____

_____

_____

_____

_____

_____

_____

_____

_____

_____

DATE ACHIEVED _____ LOCATION _____

Bucket List Goal

35

_____

WE WANT TO DO THIS BECAUSE...

_____
_____
_____

TO ACCOMPLISH THIS GOAL, WE NEED TO...

_____
_____
_____
_____

TARGET DATE _____

THOUGHTS / MEMORIES

_____
_____
_____
_____
_____
_____
_____
_____
_____
_____

DATE ACHIEVED _____ LOCATION _____

36

Bucket List Goal

_____

WE WANT TO DO THIS BECAUSE...

_____
_____
_____

TO ACCOMPLISH THIS GOAL, WE NEED TO...

_____
_____
_____
_____

TARGET DATE _____

THOUGHTS / MEMORIES

_____
_____
_____
_____
_____
_____
_____
_____
_____

DATE ACHIEVED _____ LOCATION _____

Bucket List Goal

37

WE WANT TO DO THIS BECAUSE...

_____

_____

_____

TO ACCOMPLISH THIS GOAL, WE NEED TO...

_____

_____

_____

_____

TARGET DATE _____

THOUGHTS / MEMORIES

_____

_____

_____

_____

_____

_____

_____

_____

_____

DATE ACHIEVED _____ LOCATION _____

Bucket List Goal

_____

WE WANT TO DO THIS BECAUSE...

_____

_____

_____

TO ACCOMPLISH THIS GOAL, WE NEED TO...

_____

_____

_____

_____

TARGET DATE _____

THOUGHTS / MEMORIES

_____

_____

_____

_____

_____

_____

_____

_____

_____

_____

DATE ACHIEVED _____ LOCATION _____

Bucket List Goal

39

_____

WE WANT TO DO THIS BECAUSE...

_____

_____

_____

TO ACCOMPLISH THIS GOAL, WE NEED TO...

_____

_____

_____

_____

TARGET DATE _____

THOUGHTS / MEMORIES

_____

_____

_____

_____

_____

_____

_____

_____

_____

DATE ACHIEVED _____ LOCATION _____

Bucket List Goal

_____

WE WANT TO DO THIS BECAUSE...

_____

_____

_____

TO ACCOMPLISH THIS GOAL, WE NEED TO...

_____

_____

_____

_____

TARGET DATE _____

THOUGHTS / MEMORIES

_____

_____

_____

_____

_____

_____

_____

_____

_____

_____

DATE ACHIEVED_____   LOCATION_____

Bucket List Goal

41

_____

WE WANT TO DO THIS BECAUSE...

_____
_____
_____

TO ACCOMPLISH THIS GOAL, WE NEED TO...

_____
_____
_____
_____

TARGET DATE _____

THOUGHTS / MEMORIES

_____
_____
_____
_____
_____
_____
_____
_____
_____
_____

DATE ACHIEVED _____ LOCATION _____

42

Bucket List Goal

_____

WE WANT TO DO THIS BECAUSE...

_____

_____

_____

TO ACCOMPLISH THIS GOAL, WE NEED TO...

_____

_____

_____

_____

TARGET DATE _____

THOUGHTS / MEMORIES

_____

_____

_____

_____

_____

_____

_____

_____

_____

_____

DATE ACHIEVED _____ LOCATION _____

Bucket List Goal

43

_____

WE WANT TO DO THIS BECAUSE...

_____

_____

_____

TO ACCOMPLISH THIS GOAL, WE NEED TO...

_____

_____

_____

_____

TARGET DATE _____

THOUGHTS / MEMORIES

_____

_____

_____

_____

_____

_____

_____

_____

_____

_____

DATE ACHIEVED _____ LOCATION _____

44

Bucket List Goal

_____

WE WANT TO DO THIS BECAUSE...

_____

_____

_____

TO ACCOMPLISH THIS GOAL, WE NEED TO...

_____

_____

_____

_____

TARGET DATE _____

THOUGHTS / MEMORIES

_____

_____

_____

_____

_____

_____

_____

_____

_____

_____

DATE ACHIEVED _____ LOCATION _____

Bucket List Goal

45

_____

WE WANT TO DO THIS BECAUSE...

_____

_____

_____

TO ACCOMPLISH THIS GOAL, WE NEED TO...

_____

_____

_____

_____

TARGET DATE _____

THOUGHTS / MEMORIES

_____

_____

_____

_____

_____

_____

_____

_____

_____

_____

DATE ACHIEVED _____ LOCATION _____

Bucket List Goal

_____

WE WANT TO DO THIS BECAUSE...

_____

_____

_____

TO ACCOMPLISH THIS GOAL, WE NEED TO...

_____

_____

_____

_____

TARGET DATE _____

THOUGHTS / MEMORIES

_____

_____

_____

_____

_____

_____

_____

_____

_____

DATE ACHIEVED _____ LOCATION _____

Bucket List Goal

47

_____

WE WANT TO DO THIS BECAUSE...

_____

_____

_____

TO ACCOMPLISH THIS GOAL, WE NEED TO...

_____

_____

_____

_____

TARGET DATE _____

THOUGHTS / MEMORIES

_____

_____

_____

_____

_____

_____

_____

_____

_____

DATE ACHIEVED _____ LOCATION _____

48 *Bucket List Goal*

WE WANT TO DO THIS BECAUSE...

_____

_____

_____

TO ACCOMPLISH THIS GOAL, WE NEED TO...

_____

_____

_____

_____

TARGET DATE _____

THOUGHTS / MEMORIES

_____

_____

_____

_____

_____

_____

_____

_____

_____

_____

DATE ACHIEVED _____ LOCATION _____

Bucket List Goal

49

_____

WE WANT TO DO THIS BECAUSE...

_____

_____

_____

TO ACCOMPLISH THIS GOAL, WE NEED TO...

_____

_____

_____

_____

TARGET DATE _____

THOUGHTS / MEMORIES

_____

_____

_____

_____

_____

_____

_____

_____

_____

DATE ACHIEVED _____ LOCATION _____

Bucket List Goal

_____

WE WANT TO DO THIS BECAUSE...

_____

_____

_____

TO ACCOMPLISH THIS GOAL, WE NEED TO...

_____

_____

_____

_____

TARGET DATE _____

THOUGHTS / MEMORIES

_____

_____

_____

_____

_____

_____

_____

_____

_____

_____

DATE ACHIEVED _____ LOCATION _____

Bucket List Goal

51

_____

WE WANT TO DO THIS BECAUSE...

_____

_____

_____

TO ACCOMPLISH THIS GOAL, WE NEED TO...

_____

_____

_____

_____

TARGET DATE _____

THOUGHTS / MEMORIES

_____

_____

_____

_____

_____

_____

_____

_____

_____

_____

DATE ACHIEVED _____ LOCATION _____

Bucket List Goal

52

_____

WE WANT TO DO THIS BECAUSE...

_____

_____

_____

TO ACCOMPLISH THIS GOAL, WE NEED TO...

_____

_____

_____

_____

TARGET DATE _____

THOUGHTS / MEMORIES

_____

_____

_____

_____

_____

_____

_____

_____

_____

DATE ACHIEVED _____ LOCATION _____

Bucket List Goal

53

_____

WE WANT TO DO THIS BECAUSE...

_____
_____
_____

TO ACCOMPLISH THIS GOAL, WE NEED TO...

_____
_____
_____
_____

TARGET DATE _____

THOUGHTS / MEMORIES

_____
_____
_____
_____
_____
_____
_____
_____
_____

DATE ACHIEVED _____ LOCATION _____

54

Bucket List Goal

_____

WE WANT TO DO THIS BECAUSE...

_____
_____
_____

TO ACCOMPLISH THIS GOAL, WE NEED TO...

_____
_____
_____
_____

TARGET DATE _____

THOUGHTS / MEMORIES

_____
_____
_____
_____
_____
_____
_____
_____
_____
_____

DATE ACHIEVED _____ LOCATION _____

Bucket List Goal

55

_____

WE WANT TO DO THIS BECAUSE...

_____

_____

_____

TO ACCOMPLISH THIS GOAL, WE NEED TO...

_____

_____

_____

_____

TARGET DATE _____

THOUGHTS / MEMORIES

_____

_____

_____

_____

_____

_____

_____

_____

_____

_____

DATE ACHIEVED _____ LOCATION _____

56

Bucket List Goal

_____

WE WANT TO DO THIS BECAUSE...

_____

_____

_____

TO ACCOMPLISH THIS GOAL, WE NEED TO...

_____

_____

_____

_____

TARGET DATE _____

THOUGHTS / MEMORIES

_____

_____

_____

_____

_____

_____

_____

_____

_____

_____

DATE ACHIEVED _____ LOCATION _____

Bucket List Goal

57

_____

WE WANT TO DO THIS BECAUSE...

_____
_____
_____

TO ACCOMPLISH THIS GOAL, WE NEED TO...

_____
_____
_____
_____

TARGET DATE _____

THOUGHTS / MEMORIES

_____
_____
_____
_____
_____
_____
_____
_____
_____

DATE ACHIEVED _____ LOCATION _____

Bucket List Goal

_____

WE WANT TO DO THIS BECAUSE...

_____

_____

_____

TO ACCOMPLISH THIS GOAL, WE NEED TO...

_____

_____

_____

_____

TARGET DATE _____

THOUGHTS / MEMORIES

_____

_____

_____

_____

_____

_____

_____

_____

_____

_____

DATE ACHIEVED _____ LOCATION _____

Bucket List Goal

59

_____

WE WANT TO DO THIS BECAUSE...

_____

_____

_____

TO ACCOMPLISH THIS GOAL, WE NEED TO...

_____

_____

_____

_____

TARGET DATE _____

THOUGHTS / MEMORIES

_____

_____

_____

_____

_____

_____

_____

_____

_____

DATE ACHIEVED _____ LOCATION _____

Bucket List Goal

_____

WE WANT TO DO THIS BECAUSE...

_____

_____

_____

TO ACCOMPLISH THIS GOAL, WE NEED TO...

_____

_____

_____

_____

TARGET DATE _____

THOUGHTS / MEMORIES

_____

_____

_____

_____

_____

_____

_____

_____

_____

DATE ACHIEVED _____ LOCATION _____

Bucket List Goal

61

_____

WE WANT TO DO THIS BECAUSE...

_____

_____

_____

TO ACCOMPLISH THIS GOAL, WE NEED TO...

_____

_____

_____

_____

TARGET DATE _____

THOUGHTS / MEMORIES

_____

_____

_____

_____

_____

_____

_____

_____

_____

DATE ACHIEVED _____ LOCATION _____

Bucket List Goal

_____

WE WANT TO DO THIS BECAUSE...

_____

_____

_____

TO ACCOMPLISH THIS GOAL, WE NEED TO...

_____

_____

_____

_____

TARGET DATE _____

THOUGHTS / MEMORIES

_____

_____

_____

_____

_____

_____

_____

_____

_____

DATE ACHIEVED _____ LOCATION _____

Bucket List Goal

63

_____

WE WANT TO DO THIS BECAUSE...

_____
_____
_____

TO ACCOMPLISH THIS GOAL, WE NEED TO...

_____
_____
_____
_____

TARGET DATE _____

THOUGHTS / MEMORIES

_____
_____
_____
_____
_____
_____
_____
_____
_____

DATE ACHIEVED _____ LOCATION _____

Bucket List Goal

_____

WE WANT TO DO THIS BECAUSE...

_____

_____

_____

TO ACCOMPLISH THIS GOAL, WE NEED TO...

_____

_____

_____

_____

TARGET DATE _____

THOUGHTS / MEMORIES

_____

_____

_____

_____

_____

_____

_____

_____

_____

DATE ACHIEVED _____ LOCATION _____

Bucket List Goal

65

_____

WE WANT TO DO THIS BECAUSE...

_____
_____
_____

TO ACCOMPLISH THIS GOAL, WE NEED TO...

_____
_____
_____
_____

TARGET DATE _____

THOUGHTS / MEMORIES

_____
_____
_____
_____
_____
_____
_____
_____
_____

DATE ACHIEVED _____ LOCATION _____

Bucket List Goal

_____

WE WANT TO DO THIS BECAUSE...

_____

_____

_____

TO ACCOMPLISH THIS GOAL, WE NEED TO...

_____

_____

_____

_____

TARGET DATE _____

THOUGHTS / MEMORIES

_____

_____

_____

_____

_____

_____

_____

_____

_____

_____

DATE ACHIEVED _____ LOCATION _____

Bucket List Goal

67

_____

WE WANT TO DO THIS BECAUSE...

_____
_____
_____

TO ACCOMPLISH THIS GOAL, WE NEED TO...

_____
_____
_____
_____

TARGET DATE _____

THOUGHTS / MEMORIES

_____
_____
_____
_____
_____
_____
_____
_____
_____

DATE ACHIEVED _____ LOCATION _____

Bucket List Goal

_____

WE WANT TO DO THIS BECAUSE...

_____

_____

_____

TO ACCOMPLISH THIS GOAL, WE NEED TO...

_____

_____

_____

_____

TARGET DATE _____

THOUGHTS / MEMORIES

_____

_____

_____

_____

_____

_____

_____

_____

_____

DATE ACHIEVED _____ LOCATION _____

Bucket List Goal

69

_____

WE WANT TO DO THIS BECAUSE...

_____

_____

_____

TO ACCOMPLISH THIS GOAL, WE NEED TO...

_____

_____

_____

_____

TARGET DATE _____

THOUGHTS / MEMORIES

_____

_____

_____

_____

_____

_____

_____

_____

_____

DATE ACHIEVED _____ LOCATION _____

Bucket List Goal

WE WANT TO DO THIS BECAUSE...

_____

_____

_____

TO ACCOMPLISH THIS GOAL, WE NEED TO...

_____

_____

_____

_____

TARGET DATE _____

THOUGHTS / MEMORIES

_____

_____

_____

_____

_____

_____

_____

_____

_____

DATE ACHIEVED _____ LOCATION _____

Bucket List Goal

71

_____

WE WANT TO DO THIS BECAUSE...

_____
_____
_____

TO ACCOMPLISH THIS GOAL, WE NEED TO...

_____
_____
_____
_____

TARGET DATE _____

THOUGHTS / MEMORIES

_____
_____
_____
_____
_____
_____
_____
_____
_____
_____

DATE ACHIEVED _____ LOCATION _____

72

Bucket List Goal

_____

WE WANT TO DO THIS BECAUSE...

_____

_____

_____

TO ACCOMPLISH THIS GOAL, WE NEED TO...

_____

_____

_____

_____

TARGET DATE _____

THOUGHTS / MEMORIES

_____

_____

_____

_____

_____

_____

_____

_____

_____

DATE ACHIEVED _____ LOCATION _____

Bucket List Goal

73

_____

WE WANT TO DO THIS BECAUSE...

_____
_____
_____

TO ACCOMPLISH THIS GOAL, WE NEED TO...

_____
_____
_____
_____

TARGET DATE _____

THOUGHTS / MEMORIES

_____
_____
_____
_____
_____
_____
_____
_____
_____

DATE ACHIEVED _____ LOCATION _____

74

Bucket List Goal

_____

WE WANT TO DO THIS BECAUSE...

_____
_____
_____

TO ACCOMPLISH THIS GOAL, WE NEED TO...

_____
_____
_____
_____

TARGET DATE _____

THOUGHTS / MEMORIES

_____
_____
_____
_____
_____
_____
_____
_____
_____
_____

DATE ACHIEVED _____ LOCATION _____

Bucket List Goal

75

_____

WE WANT TO DO THIS BECAUSE...

_____

_____

_____

TO ACCOMPLISH THIS GOAL, WE NEED TO...

_____

_____

_____

_____

TARGET DATE _____

THOUGHTS / MEMORIES

_____

_____

_____

_____

_____

_____

_____

_____

_____

_____

DATE ACHIEVED _____ LOCATION _____

76

Bucket List Goal

_____

WE WANT TO DO THIS BECAUSE...

_____
_____
_____

TO ACCOMPLISH THIS GOAL WE NEED TO...

_____
_____
_____
_____

TARGET DATE _____

THOUGHTS / MEMORIES

_____
_____
_____
_____
_____
_____
_____
_____
_____
_____

DATE ACHIEVED _____ LOCATION _____

Bucket List Goal

77

_____

WE WANT TO DO THIS BECAUSE...

_____

_____

_____

TO ACCOMPLISH THIS GOAL, WE NEED TO...

_____

_____

_____

_____

TARGET DATE _____

THOUGHTS / MEMORIES

_____

_____

_____

_____

_____

_____

_____

_____

_____

DATE ACHIEVED _____ LOCATION _____

Bucket List Goal

_____

WE WANT TO DO THIS BECAUSE...

_____
_____
_____

TO ACCOMPLISH THIS GOAL, WE NEED TO...

_____
_____
_____
_____

TARGET DATE _____

THOUGHTS / MEMORIES

_____
_____
_____
_____
_____
_____
_____
_____
_____
_____

DATE ACHIEVED_____   LOCATION_____

Bucket List Goal

79

_____

WE WANT TO DO THIS BECAUSE...

_____
_____
_____

TO ACCOMPLISH THIS GOAL, WE NEED TO...

_____
_____
_____
_____

TARGET DATE _____

THOUGHTS / MEMORIES

_____
_____
_____
_____
_____
_____
_____
_____
_____
_____

DATE ACHIEVED _____ LOCATION _____

80

Bucket List Goal

_____

WE WANT TO DO THIS BECAUSE...

_____

_____

_____

TO ACCOMPLISH THIS GOAL, WE NEED TO...

_____

_____

_____

_____

TARGET DATE _____

THOUGHTS / MEMORIES

_____

_____

_____

_____

_____

_____

_____

_____

_____

_____

DATE ACHIEVED _____ LOCATION _____

Bucket List Goal

81

_____

WE WANT TO DO THIS BECAUSE...

_____
_____
_____

TO ACCOMPLISH THIS GOAL, WE NEED TO...

_____
_____
_____
_____

TARGET DATE _____

THOUGHTS / MEMORIES

_____
_____
_____
_____
_____
_____
_____
_____
_____

DATE ACHIEVED _____ LOCATION _____

82

Bucket List Goal

_____

WE WANT TO DO THIS BECAUSE...

_____
_____
_____
_____

TO ACCOMPLISH THIS GOAL, WE NEED TO...

_____
_____
_____
_____

TARGET DATE _____

THOUGHTS / MEMORIES

_____
_____
_____
_____
_____
_____
_____
_____
_____
_____

DATE ACHIEVED _____ LOCATION _____

Bucket List Goal

83

_____

WE WANT TO DO THIS BECAUSE...

_____
_____
_____

TO ACCOMPLISH THIS GOAL, WE NEED TO...

_____
_____
_____
_____

TARGET DATE _____

THOUGHTS / MEMORIES

_____
_____
_____
_____
_____
_____
_____
_____
_____
_____

DATE ACHIEVED _____ LOCATION _____

84

Bucket List Goal

_____

WE WANT TO DO THIS BECAUSE...

_____
_____
_____

TO ACCOMPLISH THIS GOAL, WE NEED TO...

_____
_____
_____
_____

TARGET DATE _____

THOUGHTS / MEMORIES

_____
_____
_____
_____
_____
_____
_____
_____
_____
_____

DATE ACHIEVED _____ LOCATION _____

Bucket List Goal

85

_____

WE WANT TO DO THIS BECAUSE...

_____
_____
_____

TO ACCOMPLISH THIS GOAL, WE NEED TO...

_____
_____
_____
_____

TARGET DATE _____

THOUGHTS / MEMORIES

_____
_____
_____
_____
_____
_____
_____
_____
_____

DATE ACHIEVED _____ LOCATION _____

86

Bucket List Goal

_____

WE WANT TO DO THIS BECAUSE...

_____

_____

_____

TO ACCOMPLISH THIS GOAL, WE NEED TO...

_____

_____

_____

_____

TARGET DATE _____

THOUGHTS / MEMORIES

_____

_____

_____

_____

_____

_____

_____

_____

_____

_____

DATE ACHIEVED _____ LOCATION _____

Bucket List Goal

87

_____

WE WANT TO DO THIS BECAUSE...

_____

_____

_____

TO ACCOMPLISH THIS GOAL, WE NEED TO...

_____

_____

_____

_____

TARGET DATE _____

THOUGHTS / MEMORIES

_____

_____

_____

_____

_____

_____

_____

_____

_____

DATE ACHIEVED _____ LOCATION _____

Bucket List Goal

_____

WE WANT TO DO THIS BECAUSE...

_____
_____
_____

TO ACCOMPLISH THIS GOAL, WE NEED TO...

_____
_____
_____
_____

TARGET DATE _____

THOUGHTS / MEMORIES

_____
_____
_____
_____
_____
_____
_____
_____
_____

DATE ACHIEVED _____ LOCATION _____

Bucket List Goal

89

WE WANT TO DO THIS BECAUSE...

_____

_____

_____

TO ACCOMPLISH THIS GOAL, WE NEED TO...

_____

_____

_____

_____

TARGET DATE _____

THOUGHTS / MEMORIES

_____

_____

_____

_____

_____

_____

_____

_____

_____

_____

DATE ACHIEVED _____ LOCATION _____

90

Bucket List Goal

_____

WE WANT TO DO THIS BECAUSE...

_____

_____

_____

TO ACCOMPLISH THIS GOAL, WE NEED TO...

_____

_____

_____

_____

TARGET DATE _____

THOUGHTS / MEMORIES

_____

_____

_____

_____

_____

_____

_____

_____

_____

_____

DATE ACHIEVED _____ LOCATION _____

Bucket List Goal

91

_____

WE WANT TO DO THIS BECAUSE...

_____
_____
_____

TO ACCOMPLISH THIS GOAL, WE NEED TO...

_____
_____
_____
_____

TARGET DATE _____

THOUGHTS / MEMORIES

_____
_____
_____
_____
_____
_____
_____
_____
_____

DATE ACHIEVED _____ LOCATION _____

92 Bucket List Goal

_____

WE WANT TO DO THIS BECAUSE...

_____
_____
_____

TO ACCOMPLISH THIS GOAL, WE NEED TO...

_____
_____
_____
_____

TARGET DATE _____

THOUGHTS / MEMORIES

_____
_____
_____
_____
_____
_____
_____
_____
_____
_____

DATE ACHIEVED _____ LOCATION _____

Bucket List Goal

93

_____

WE WANT TO DO THIS BECAUSE...

_____
_____
_____

TO ACCOMPLISH THIS GOAL, WE NEED TO...

_____
_____
_____
_____

TARGET DATE _____

THOUGHTS / MEMORIES

_____
_____
_____
_____
_____
_____
_____
_____
_____

DATE ACHIEVED _____ LOCATION _____

Bucket List Goal

94

_____

WE WANT TO DO THIS BECAUSE...

_____
_____
_____

TO ACCOMPLISH THIS GOAL, WE NEED TO...

_____
_____
_____
_____

TARGET DATE _____

THOUGHTS / MEMORIES

_____
_____
_____
_____
_____
_____
_____
_____
_____
_____

DATE ACHIEVED _____ LOCATION _____

Bucket List Goal

95

_____

WE WANT TO DO THIS BECAUSE...

_____
_____
_____

TO ACCOMPLISH THIS GOAL, WE NEED TO...

_____
_____
_____
_____

TARGET DATE _____

THOUGHTS / MEMORIES

_____
_____
_____
_____
_____
_____
_____
_____
_____

DATE ACHIEVED _____ LOCATION _____

Bucket List Goal

_____

WE WANT TO DO THIS BECAUSE...

_____

_____

_____

TO ACCOMPLISH THIS GOAL, WE NEED TO...

_____

_____

_____

_____

TARGET DATE _____

THOUGHTS / MEMORIES

_____

_____

_____

_____

_____

_____

_____

_____

_____

DATE ACHIEVED _____ LOCATION _____

Bucket List Goal

97

_____

WE WANT TO DO THIS BECAUSE...

_____

_____

_____

TO ACCOMPLISH THIS GOAL, WE NEED TO...

_____

_____

_____

_____

TARGET DATE _____

THOUGHTS / MEMORIES

_____

_____

_____

_____

_____

_____

_____

_____

_____

_____

DATE ACHIEVED _____ LOCATION _____

98

Bucket List Goal

_____

WE WANT TO DO THIS BECAUSE...

_____

_____

_____

TO ACCOMPLISH THIS GOAL, WE NEED TO...

_____

_____

_____

_____

TARGET DATE _____

THOUGHTS / MEMORIES

_____

_____

_____

_____

_____

_____

_____

_____

_____

_____

DATE ACHIEVED _____ LOCATION _____

Bucket List Goal

99

_____

WE WANT TO DO THIS BECAUSE...

_____

_____

_____

TO ACCOMPLISH THIS GOAL, WE NEED TO...

_____

_____

_____

_____

TARGET DATE _____

THOUGHTS / MEMORIES

_____

_____

_____

_____

_____

_____

_____

_____

_____

_____

DATE ACHIEVED _____ LOCATION _____

Bucket List Goal

_____

WE WANT TO DO THIS BECAUSE...

_____
_____
_____

TO ACCOMPLISH THIS GOAL, WE NEED TO...

_____
_____
_____
_____

TARGET DATE _____

THOUGHTS / MEMORIES

_____
_____
_____
_____
_____
_____
_____
_____
_____
_____

DATE ACHIEVED _____ LOCATION _____

NOTES

NOTES

NOTES

NOTES

NOTES

NOTES

Made in the USA
Monee, IL
26 November 2023

47400154R10063